Prosperity
Every Day

Prosperity Every Day

*A Daily Companion on Your Journey
to Greater Wealth and Happiness*

JULIA CAMERON
WITH EMMA LIVELY

JEREMY P. TARCHER/PENGUIN
a member of Penguin Group (USA)
New York

JEREMY P. TARCHER/PENGUIN
Published by the Penguin Group
Penguin Group (USA) LLC
375 Hudson Street
New York, New York 10014

USA · Canada · UK · Ireland · Australia
New Zealand · India · South Africa · China

penguin.com
A Penguin Random House Company

Most Tarcher/Penguin books are available at special quantity discounts for bulk
purchase for sales promotions, premiums, fund-raising, and educational needs.
Special books or book excerpts also can be created to fit specific needs.
For details, write: Special.Markets@us.penguingroup.com.

Library of Congress Cataloging-in-Publication Data

Cameron, Julia.
Prosperity every day : a daily companion on your journey to greater wealth
and happiness / Julia Cameron, Emma Lively.
p.   cm.
ISBN 978-0-399-16918-2
1. Self-actualization (Psychology).   2. Finance, Personal.   3. Happiness.
4. Spiritual life.   I. Lively, Emma.   II. Title.
BF637.S4C3417   2015   2014035316
158.1—dc23

Printed in the United States of America
1   3   5   7   9   10   8   6   4   2

BOOK DESIGN BY AMANDA DEWEY

This book is dedicated to Joel Fotinos,
for his faith and guidance

ACKNOWLEDGMENTS

Sara Carder
Valerie Green
Gerard Hackett
Susan Raihofer

Author's Note

People think of prosperity as a fiscal bottom line. "When I have X amount of money, I will feel better." The truth is that prosperity is a spiritual bottom line, and the formula should actually be: "When I have X amount of faith, I will feel better."

—*from* The Prosperous Heart

True prosperity has nothing to do with money. And no matter where you are financially, you can feel better immediately. Yes, we are going to take steps to resolve concrete financial questions along the way. But it's not necessary to wait until some undetermined moment in the future to appreciate the life you have. If you decide you should wait until you are rich "enough" to feel like you have "enough," you will never get there.

When we shift our perspective to one of gratitude, we instantly feel better. When we feel better, our attitude toward ourselves—and others—is naturally more generous. More generous, we prosper.

Drawing from multiple sources, this book is intended as a daily support on your journey toward greater prosperity—in your wallet and in your life. Read daily, these meditations will put you on a spiritual path that improves your solvency. Deceptively simple, these meditations perform a spiritual realignment.

GLOSSARY OF
BASIC CONCEPTS

COUNTING: a daily tabulation of monies in and monies out

MONEY MAP: a monthly tabulation of our cash flow

PROSPERITY PLAN: a map of where we feel our money should go

ABSTINENCE: no debting

CREDIT CARD ROULETTE: maxing out one card and moving to the next

SOLVENCY: a state of financial security; we have "enough"

MONEY MADNESS: a state of the misuse of money characterized by debting and overspending

SPIRIT: the spiritual source of our well-being

Prosperity
Every Day

January

A Spiritual Bottom Line

Prosperity isn't about money. This statement flies in the face of our usual thinking. "Of course prosperity is about money," we want to say. But if we believe prosperity is about money, then there is never enough. We need to recognize that prosperity is a spiritual bottom line, not a fiscal one.

JANUARY 2

Unlimited Supply

When we are grounded spiritually, we recognize that Spirit is our source. This means we have an unlimited supply. Turning to a spiritual source moves us into a feeling of abundance. There is one energy, one force, sustaining all of life. That source is Spirit.

JANUARY 3

Money and Creativity

Many of us believe we will be more creative when we are financially comfortable. "When I have enough money, then I'll try . . ." we tell ourselves. But creativity does not depend on money. It depends on our sense of abundance. When we extend ourselves creatively, we often trigger an increased flow financially. Creativity is an act of faith. We extend ourselves, believing that good will come to pass. This act of faith brings us closer to our Creator, closer to our flow of good.

JANUARY 4

Having Enough

We are often anxious, telling ourselves that our security is in jeopardy. We fret and worry rather than take concrete actions to remedy our situation. Counting is the beginning of security. We learn how much money we have and where it goes. We are ending fiscal vagueness. As our knowledge becomes more concrete, we are better able to act on our own behalf. It helps to remind ourselves that we have always been taken care of. The Universe is abundant, and it manifests its abundance in many ways.

January 5

Clarity

Putting pen to page and recording our spending and earning gives us the beginning of clarity. Prosperity is not about vagueness, a dim sense that we have enough. Rather, prosperity and clarity go hand in hand. We don't think we might have enough; we know we do have enough. And if we have a shortfall, we know its proportions. We gain clarity about what we can do to improve our solvency. Often, it is a small step. Are we billing properly for our time and attention? If not, we are debting to ourselves.

January 6

Anxiety

Anxiety blocks our flow. Worried about what we don't have, focused on our lack, our anxiety increases. It takes a deliberate act of faith to reverse our scarcity thinking. Often, work with an affirmation will clear a channel. The affirmation can be simple: "There is plenty for all of us, including myself."

January 7

Adrenaline

Many of us, seeking prosperity, find ourselves facing resistance. Why? We have an active addiction to anxiety. We are accustomed to worry. We are habituated to an overflow of adrenaline. Ambiguity is the breeding ground of obsession—but Counting eliminates ambiguity.

January 8

Spirit as Source

When we rely on a higher power, we invite a divine energy to enter our lives. No longer self-reliant, we rely instead on the limitless abundance that is our true source. No task is too difficult for divine intelligence. As we allow Spirit's mind to think through us, problems are replaced with solutions.

JANUARY 9

Addiction

Addiction saps our energy. It keeps us from feeling abundant. Addiction can take many forms: alcohol, drugs, sex and love addiction, overwork—any of these can divert our flow or block it entirely. Turning to our higher power for help with our addictions leads us to freedom and prosperity.

JANUARY 10

A Beautiful Harvest

Solvent, we plant the seeds of a beautiful harvest. We look forward with anticipation to the bounty that will come. We count our blessings and know that more abundance follows. Taking our cue from the natural world, we expect abundance.

True Values

For many of us, values translate into material belongings. We want the new car, the designer clothes, the chic apartment. So focused are we on these goals that we seldom ask, "What do I truly value?" Our true values, often neglected, are spiritual. We want to feel comfortable in our own skin, secure—something we tell ourselves material goods will convey. The truth is that our spiritual well-being comes to us as we express our true values, extending ourselves in generosity to others.

January 12

Loss

When we experience material loss, we often find ourselves shaken in our faith. "How could Spirit let that happen?" we ask, when we should be asking, "Where does this loss point me?" Very often, we are encountering gain disguised as loss. A blow to our economic well-being asks us to acknowledge that in the moment, we are actually fine, despite our loss. We are asked to redouble our faith, affirming that Spirit is in charge and that there is a divine plan of goodness for us, of which this loss is a part. We can pray for acceptance. We can ask to see the silver lining. We can ask to trust that such a lining always exists.

JANUARY 13

Spiritual Nutrients

Sourced in Spirit, we are each abloom in the garden of God. Unique and irreplaceable, we are cared for precisely. We are each given the specific spiritual nutrients that result in our glorious blossoming.

January 14

The Magic Number

Many of us have a magic number, a sum that we tell ourselves will solve all of our problems. The magic number is elusive. It is always more than we currently have. And yet, when we reach our magic number, we often find that it has gone up. Our expenses have gone up as well. Our magic number is a fantasy. We tell ourselves our finances will be manageable when . . . but financial manageability is grounded in what we have got, not what we will have. It is often the imagined status our magic number will confer that is our true addiction. "If I make six figures, everyone will respect me," we falsely believe.

January 15

Abundance for All

We commit ourselves to Spirit. Doing so, we open our hearts and our minds to all of creation. Rather than having a separate, selfish voice, we find ourselves united to all. Rejoicing in our abundance, we see abundance for all.

January 16

Turbulent Emotions

As we withdraw from money madness, we often experience turbulent emotions. Committed to change, we ride those emotions out. Eventually, always, serenity takes their place.

JANUARY 17

Our Creative Dreams

Too often, we tell ourselves that our creative dreams are beyond our reach. If we had more money, we would be more creative, we say. We have it exactly backwards. If we are more creative, we experience a greater flow. When we take our dreams to our higher power and ask for them to manifest, we are often led, a step at a time, to their fulfillment.

January 18

A Habit of Debting

Some of us have a habit of debting. We borrow from friends and family. We run up our credit cards. We borrow ahead on paychecks. As a rule, we live beyond our means. Amassing debt, we are stealing from our future, for when future monies arrive, they have already been spent.

Risk

We tell ourselves that risk is dangerous, and yet, no risk is more dangerous. When we cling to our known life, we deny ourselves the chance for expansion. A habit of risk—small risk building upon small risk—prepares us to meet opportunity with optimism.

JANUARY 20

Expansion

"Will I feel better or worse for having tried expansion?" Often, we find we can survive a risk that doesn't pan out more easily than we can survive no risk at all. "Why not try it," the daring heart ventures. Often, when we try the risk at hand, the silver lining is revealed.

Gratitude

Ours is an abundant Universe. We come to believe this through the practice of gratitude. As we count our blessings, our blessings seem to multiply. As we express our gratitude for all that we have, we become able to receive more. Blessings build on blessings. By focusing on the positive, we open the door to abundance.

Daily Gratitude

The Prosperous Heart is a grateful heart, focused on blessings, not on lack. A daily practice of gratitude helps us to cherish and husband what we have. We may begin with the basics: I am grateful for my health. Next, we might add: I am grateful for my health, and that I didn't catch the cold that seems to be going around. A gratitude list builds upon itself.

JANUARY 23

The Gratitude List

Gratitude builds upon gratitude. At first, our list might be five items. Before long, it will be ten, then twenty, then twenty-five. Our gratitude list shows us we are being taken care of. We are comforted by our list. We are made to feel secure.

JANUARY 24

Clutter

A serene environment makes for serene thinking. A cluttered environment causes our thinking to be scattered. Chaos breeds chaos. Serenity breeds serenity. The choice is ours. How do we choose to live? Most meditation practices emphasize twenty minutes as an ideal. A daily twenty minutes, put to de-cluttering, leaves us with a sense of spiritual well-being and expansion.

JANUARY 25

A Money History

Tracing our money history, we often find patterns set in motion by our childhoods. We may have grown up learning that money equaled love. We may have learned that we must work hard for money, causing us to be miserly as adults. Money may be equated with self-worth. We may have learned that rich equaled smart and poor equaled dumb. We may have learned to live beyond our means, or to borrow with little thought of repayment. For most of us, money is symbolic as well as tangible.

Anger

Anger is one of the keys to prosperity. Anger is a tough-love friend. It tells us when we have been betrayed, and when we have betrayed ourselves. Anger is a signal that our boundaries have been trespassed upon. Anger asks us to take action on our own behalf. Sometimes, anger asks that we undertake a difficult conversation, spelling out precisely how we have felt violated. Sometimes anger asks that we make an inner resolve: "I will never do *that* again." Anger is a map. It points us in the direction of our true values.

Velocity

Ours is a fast-paced society. We rush pell-mell, hurrying to reach our goals. This frantic pace wears us out. We have no faith in Spirit's timing. Ironically, when we slow down, the rewards in our life seem to speed up. As we attune ourselves to the Universe's pacing, we are able to take advantage of the many opportunities that come our way.

January 28

Out of Debt

When we debt, we are compromising our future. When we stop debting, we experience greater freedom. The cash flow that we have is ours to spend creatively. When we are not mortgaged to our debts, we are free to dream, and to act in the direction of our dreams. Undistracted by the weight of our debts, our imagination can turn from the negative to the positive.

January 29

Friendship

The experience of prosperity is one of security and safety. Pivotal to this experience is having a sound and sober inner circle. We choose our friends wisely. Their solvency reinforces our own.

A Debt-Free Life

It pays us—a telling phrase—to survey our debting behaviors and to make a plan to live within our means
one day at a time. Breaking the vicious cycle of debt
gives us self-worth, although at first, a life without
debt may seem impossible. A day at a time, a debt-free
life can be ours.

JANUARY 31

Community

As we prosper, we lose our sense of alienation. Owing no one, we are free to forge the bonds of community. Responsible to ourselves and to others, we are trustworthy. Others are attracted to us as never before.

February

FEBRUARY 1

Slipping

When we slip up on Counting, we often say, "What's
the use?" and go on a full-fledged spending binge. We
don't realize we can simply start anew. But we can pick
up where we are and jump back in. Our solvency tools
are always ready and waiting for us.

Taking Action

Solvency is not static. When we are solvent, we are able to prosper. This requires positive actions on our own behalf. We are not hamstrung by debt. As we refrain from acquiring debt a day at a time, we are taking a positive action. Not debting is an action. It frees us to move in the direction of our dreams.

FEBRUARY 3

Divine Assistance

We are constantly mentored by Spirit. We are led carefully and well. There is no situation too tangled and complex that Spirit cannot find a solution. As we ask for help, we are given divine assistance. Divine intelligence leads us to right action.

February 4

Mentors

Many of us grow up with no financial education. Our parents do not teach us fiscal tools. They may not have them themselves. In striving for a sense of prosperity, it is important we find financial mentors, people who are comfortable "talking money," people for whom money is a tool and not a master.

A Silver Lining

When we make a commitment to align ourselves with Spirit, Spirit makes a commitment back to us. We will be safe, sheltered, and secure under Spirit's protection. If we do encounter adversity, Spirit will turn it to opportunity, revealing an often-unexpected silver lining if we are willing to look for it.

FEBRUARY 6

Cash Flow

The panicky feeling that comes with feeling broke can usefully be reframed. If you are owed monies in, you're not really broke. You have a cash flow problem. Your financial mentor might suggest you hire a lawyer to pursue accounts receivable. At all times, your mentor will act—and urge you to act—as if you have self-esteem, whether you feel panicked or not.

FEBRUARY 7

Adventure

The Prosperous Heart is an adventurous heart. It is not stuck in a rut; rather, it moves in new directions, acting on its curiosities. Freed from debt, we are free to dream. Acting on those dreams in concrete form gives us an experience of optimism and strength. As we expand our horizons, we experience the power of a benevolent "Something," which many people come to call Spirit.

Never Alone

When our finances are precarious, many of us experience a sense of alienation. We feel alone. We feel no one can understand our pressures. Our stress haunts us and is a constant companion. As we work to achieve solvency, we begin to feel the world is a benevolent place. Instead of isolation, we feel a sense of connection. We are a part of a greater whole.

Self-Kindness

Although we seldom recognize it, fiscal irresponsibility is a form of cruelty to ourselves. As we debt, we invite stress into our lives. We dodge phone calls from bill collectors. We avoid opening our mail. We play credit card roulette, maxing out one card and moving on to another. Our expenses exceed our earnings. A nagging self-loathing becomes a constant soundtrack darkening our days. As we work to achieve solvency, living within our means, we experience a new sensation: self-love. Fiscal responsibility is an act of loving kindness toward ourselves.

February 10

Unlimited Abundance

When my finances are grounded in Spirit, I see a world of beauty all around me. The primrose, the kitten, the lily, the fern, the maple, the willow, the moss on a tree trunk near a mountain stream—all these sights and many more speak to me of Spirit's unlimited abundance.

Spirit in Action

Divine intelligence flows through the Universe. Divine wisdom is ours for the asking. As we rely upon Spirit for guidance in all things, our guidance comes to us in many forms. It may be internal: the still, small voice, the hunch. It may be external: the coincidence, the stranger's conversation overheard. Guidance comes to us as synchronicity. We "happen" to be in the right place at the right time. Our intuition leads us. Its promptings are Spirit in action.

An Expansive Destiny

Sourced in Spirit and connected through Spirit to all of life, the Prosperous Heart receives guidance to expand. In expanding, it fulfills its destiny.

February 13

Boundaries

The Prosperous Heart is a generous heart. Free from the burden of debt or manic spending, we experience the security of healthy boundaries. Ironically, having good boundaries allows us to extend ourselves on behalf of others. We do not debt by offering loans we cannot afford when we know what we can afford to offer.

FEBRUARY 14

A Freshening Breeze

Counting, we experience a freshening breeze that relieves our financial torment. The breath of Spirit carries solutions. Our problems become mere questions to which Spirit knows the answers.

Listening

The Prosperous Heart is free to listen for guidance. The still, small voice becomes amplified. We find ourselves guided and guarded. Placing our affairs in the hands of a higher wisdom, we attune ourselves to new directions that are divinely orchestrated. The hunch or inspiration gradually becomes a working part of our mind. We are led carefully and well.

Saying "Yes"

The first fruit of Counting is accountability. We know where our money comes from and where our money goes. We are freed from ambiguity and vagueness. We have a solid foundation on which to build our lives. This foundation allows us to say "yes" to the Universe. We are freed to be positive and optimistic. We are freed to spend along the lines of our true values. We are freed to say "yes" to life.

Immersed in Spirit

I am within Spirit and Spirit is within me. I am immersed at all times within divine life. Divine intelligence leads me forward. Spirit thinks through me, illuminating my path.

FEBRUARY 18

Forgiving Ourselves

If Counting is the first step toward solvency, it is also the first step toward self-forgiveness. Putting our finances in black and white, we achieve clarity and dignity. We are not our debts. We can learn to spend more wisely and to have compassion for the self who abused our finances. After all, we were fueled by fear—fear that we were not enough without grandiose spending We can forgive ourselves. We are not our debts.

February 19

Inner Resource

The strength of Spirit is without limit. When I turn to Spirit within, I tap a limitless inner resource. Reliant upon Spirit, I experience strength. In my quest for solvency, I am aided and guided.

February 20

Dismantling Negativity

Negativity has no place in the Prosperous Heart. As we place our affairs in the hands of higher wisdom, we relinquish our attempts at control. New and more positive perspectives are afforded to us. We are freed from fear and anxiety. As we come to sense the safety and security of divine order, we are able to let go of our fearful projections.

Spirit's Plan

Spirit is a large and harmonious energy. It pours its blessings over all of life. As we consciously choose to open our hearts to Spirit, we become instruments of the divine will. Our solvency is part of Spirit's plan for us.

A Bright Future

Counting its blessings for all already received, confident that more blessings will be forthcoming, the Prosperous Heart has feelings of abundance. Safe and secure in its bond with Spirit, it looks to the future with optimism.

Moving Forward

Counting enables us to move forward. Freed from the stress of self-abusive spending, we are able to spend along the lines of our true values. We are able to move in the direction of our dreams. We have the humility necessary to start small. We no longer chase the "big deal." Instead, following our Prosperity Plan, we move forward one small, yet solid, step at a time.

FEBRUARY 24

The Melody of Life

When we are solvent, our lives are harmonious. Each of us becomes a true note, contributing our joyous sound to the melody of life. Our song is one of freedom and expansion.

Pacing

Our world is a rushed and hurried place. We often believe we must go faster as the world around us goes
pell-mell. We frequently argue with Spirit over the
pacing of events. We want what we want, and we want
it now. The Prosperous Heart learns to rely upon Spirit's timing. Taking a cue from the natural world, it
trusts the seasons of events.

Procrastination

Procrastination is a side effect of perfectionism. Afraid that we cannot do something perfectly, we hang back from trying at all. Often, we call procrastination laziness, but it is not laziness. It is fear. As we learn to dismantle our perfectionism, we find ourselves free to move ahead. Our procrastination yields to baby steps in the direction of our dreams.

The Relief of Harmony

Life without solvency is a life of dissonance. Our needs and desires clash with those around us. We are out of sorts and out of tune. Turning to Spirit, we experience relief. We experience harmony. Our days are filled with the music of Spirit's love.

Spirit's Leading

When we trust Spirit as the source of our good, we find ourselves led by cues and prompting, both internal and external. Focused on the positive, we find ourselves led to more peace, more prosperity, and more joy.

FEBRUARY 29

Slowing Down

Anger is a "tough-love friend." We feel anger when our values have been trod upon by ourselves or others. Often, anger is linked with jealousy: Someone else has gone further and faster than we have. It's not fair, we fume, refusing to look at our own participation in the situation. Did I work on my play? Did I rehearse my monologue? Did I Count today? Did I spend within my Prosperity Plan? In short, was I responsible to myself and my dreams?

March

MARCH 1

Living in the Now

Counting enables us to live in the now. We are not trapped by our past behaviors, and we are not afraid of our futures. We stop saying, "Maybe tomorrow . . ." as we focus on what we are able to do today.

March 2

Obsession

The Prosperous Heart is freed from obsession. Freed from grandiose schemes that we use to medicate our low self-worth, we no longer believe in the "big deal"—that grand "something" that will prove our worth. We have a sense of our self as worthy, a feeling divorced from our financial bottom line. We no longer need to obsess about what it will be like "when . . ." Instead, we value the day we are in.

MARCH 3

Security

As we become secure in our finances, we are able to experience greater security in our friendships. We no longer seek to be rescued or to rescue. Freed from unspoken demands, our friendships become reciprocal.

MARCH 4

Humility

As we place our lives in the care of a higher power, we practice humility. There is a higher hand than our own steering our affairs. As we open our minds to guidance from this higher source, we become right-sized. No longer playing God, we are able to receive guidance.

MARCH 5

Spirit's Timing

Committed to solvency, we become attuned to the tempo Spirit intends for us. Rather than fight with Spirit over timing, we take our cue from the natural world and allow seasons to evolve naturally.

MARCH 6

Honoring Others

We prosper ourselves and others when we express generosity in small ways—the smile at the checkout counter, holding open the door for an elderly woman, helping someone to cross the street—these are all acts of generosity. Generosity is a spiritual choice. We take the time to honor others.

MARCH 7

Abundant Supply

Prosperity is grounded in generosity. We trust that there is an abundant Universe. We trust that there is enough for us to share. Many of us unconsciously believe the Universe is a stingy place and we must hoard our assets. As we learn to focus on the generosity of the Universe, as we learn to recognize Spirit as the source, we begin to have a sense of abundant supply. This supply can be shared. There is always more.

March 8

Gentle Guidance

The Prosperous Heart is freed from the static of fearful anxiety. Instead, it is tuned to a higher frequency. Sourced in Spirit, it listens for the "still, small voice." Guidance makes itself known gently and quietly.

MARCH 9

Asking for Money

For many of us, money is a taboo subject, something we would rather not mention, something that we wish would straighten itself out without our having to take action. Yet a first step toward solvency is the ability to talk about money as a neutral topic, to ask for monies owed us without a sense of guilt or anxiety. Monies owed us is a fact, and we need not attach shame or embarrassment to asking for what is rightly ours.

MARCH 10

A Higher Plan

If we have placed our finances in the hands of a higher power, we need to trust when work is scarce that there is a higher plan. We often think that we are fine when paychecks come in a timely fashion. But Spirit's timing may differ from our own wishes, and so we must learn to accept Spirit's timing, knowing that we are safe in this higher plan.

Taking Action

We must work to trust that we are fine when monies are not forthcoming. Sometimes we need to take action. Some debts require a timely email reminder. Others may require a lawyer. Our willingness to speak up on our own behalf is a part of solvency. Sometimes, the actions we must take are spiritual. A heartfelt prayer, a decision to trust Spirit, is what is called for.

MARCH 12

Competition

Competition is grounded in scarcity thinking. There is enough for one winner, we believe, and not enough for all. The truth is, there is enough for all of us. We need not compete with each other. We need only focus on our own growth and expansion.

MARCH 13

Jealousy

Jealousy is a map. It tells us the direction we wish to go. Frequently accompanied by anger, it points us in the direction of our dreams. Many times we discover our dreams through jealousy. We prosper when we can find the wisdom in our jealousy and heed its advice.

MARCH 14

Media Deprivation

Few tools are more effective than Media Deprivation. Media Deprivation? That's right. No emails, no reading, no talk radio. When we declare a "time-out" from the hectic pace of our lives, the ease and clarity of our insights may surprise us.

Manifestation

When we place our dependency on Spirit, we find ourselves safe and secure. Spirit dreams through us, manifesting our dreams in a powerful yet peaceful unfolding.

MARCH 16

Further Education

When we place our affairs in the hands of a higher power, we are often led to seek further knowledge. Call it "doing the footwork"—our willingness to educate ourselves regarding our options can bring us to a state of calm. Seeking the guidance of mentors, we may learn to have a quiet acceptance regarding our finances. A little education may show us there is no need to panic.

MARCH 17

Spirit's Gifts

We are all the cherished children of Spirit, each unique and irreplaceable, original and powerful. Spirit gifts us with these things. As we come to financial clarity, we can use these gifts for our good.

MARCH 18

The Money Map

One of the first fruits of Counting is clarity. Our money is a map. Tracing our spending, we become aware of our values. Often, we find out we are spending not according to our true values. Counting shows us where we need to make corrections. We often learn that we do have "enough," but that we have been misappropriating. The dime—or the dollar—spent according to our actual values leaves us with a feeling of abundance.

MARCH 19

The Next Right Thing

In twelve-step programs, it is often remarked that God is an acronym for "Good, Orderly Direction." Praying for knowledge of Spirit's will for us and the power to carry it out, we are often led in tiny increments. While we cannot change the big picture in one fell swoop, we can do the next right thing. It may be something as simple as sorting the mail. Clutter and clarity cannot coexist.

MARCH 20

Never Too Late

There is no situation too complex to yield to the touch of the higher power. We often feel it's "too late" to seek help. But spiritual help is available to us at all times. All that is required is the humility to ask for help. Alert attention can then show us that our problems hold solutions. A higher power is a generous energy. The outworking of our problems gives Spirit pleasure.

The Prosperity Plan

Counting tells us where our money goes. A Prosperity Plan based on our Counting tells us how we can optimally adjust our spending. A Prosperity Plan holds categories for self-nurturing. Food, clothes, entertainment—all may need an adjustment of our cash flow. If we have a twice-daily Starbucks habit, we have more than enough money for a film. A Prosperity Plan is a sketch. We are outlining our ideal spending. As we spend in ways appropriate to our values, we feel increased self-worth.

MARCH 22

A Divine Plan of Goodness

There is a divine plan of goodness for each of us. Rather than living a life of hardship, we are freed, through solvency, to lead a life of grace. Good flows to us from many unexpected directions. Sourced in Spirit, we prosper.

MARCH 23

Volunteerism

The Prosperous Heart is generous. It seeks ways to give without always demanding cash on the barrelhead. Volunteerism gives us a sense of our value as we choose in what format our giving can best be done. From hospice work to literacy programs, there is a wide variety of need. As we take an inventory of our own skills, we find we can match needs to assets.

MARCH 24

Inner Promptings

As we open our hearts to a higher power, we learn that our guidance is trustworthy. Gradually, we develop faith in our inner promptings. We are within Spirit and Spirit is within us. We do know right action.

Safe Companions

Often, we pick up the emotional coloration of those around us. For this reason, we must be vigilant about surrounding ourselves with safe companions, those whose values match our own. If we seek to improve our spiritual life, we must surround ourselves with believers, not skeptics. If we want to trust in a benevolent Universe, we must seek out people who have optimism and faith.

MARCH 26

Asking for Guidance

All of us contain a source of inner wisdom. We each have the capacity to ask for—and receive—guidance from this source. A simple way to ask for guidance is to take pen to paper, writing, "Help! What should I do about ___?" and then listening for the answer to form. Very often, our guidance is simple yet profound. A habit of daily writing yields us a well-lit path. We are well and carefully led. We need only ask for guidance and pause to receive it.

A Lantern of Goodness

Spirit is a lantern of goodness. It illuminates our path, shining its bright light into the nooks and crannies of our experience. All is well, it assures us as it pours forth the graceful good into our lives. Committed to Spirit, we find our lives lightened.

MARCH 28

Receiving Abundance

When we count our blessings, they seem to multiply. The more we give thanks for what we have, the more we are able to receive. The Universe is abundant; our job is to recognize and receive that abundance.

MARCH 29

Becoming Original

As we turn within, seeking guidance, we tap into the flow of divine ideas. Spirit's originality is limitless, and as we allow our own minds and hearts to open, Spirit thinks through us, so we become original.

MARCH 30

Electing Optimism

Optimism is an elected attitude. We have a choice, always, between faith and fear. As we choose faith, we practice optimism—a belief that all is well despite appearances to the contrary.

MARCH 31

Humor

Life is a serious business, many of us feel. We carry tension and stress as a badge of virtue. And yet, we have no proof that hardship brings us what we want. The natural world is our teacher—the butterfly lighting on a rose, the squirrel flirting with its tail, the kitten enchanted by a ball of string. There is humor to be found in all these things.

April

APRIL 1

Joy

The Prosperous Heart is joyful. Trusting that all is in divine order, trusting that the Universe is benevolent and that the future holds much good, a joyful heart lives in peace and prosperity. It enthusiastically anticipates success, believing that its endeavors will prosper.

Faith

Placing our affairs in the hands of a higher wisdom is an act of faith. We believe in divine intelligence, and we believe that we are guided by that intelligence. There is no problem too large or too complex to be solved and resolved by Spirit.

APRIL 3

Spirit's Seasons

The Prosperous Heart believes in Spirit's timing. There is no sense of rush or strain, no feeling of urgency or emergency. Instead, the Prosperous Heart believes in Spirit's seasons. There is a time for planting, gestation, nurturance, and harvest. Growth is not forced. There is time enough for all things to come to fruition and prosper.

APRIL 4

Pleasure

Spirit intends us to have pleasure. This world is Spirit's gift to us: bountiful and beautiful. As we take delight in creation, the Creator delights in our pleasure.

APRIL 5

Forgiving Others

As we become firmly rooted in solvency, we gain compassion for our fearful former selves. We gain compassion, too, for others who suffer from unmanageable finances. After all, we were recently among their ranks. Solvent, we give them our greatest gift as we live by example.

APRIL 6

Inspiration

Inspiration is a gift of the Prosperous Heart. Taking the time to seek guidance, learning to recognize the "still, small voice," hearing the higher harmonic of inspiration, is a learned skill. The daily practice of prayer and meditation, often expressed throughout the day in "time-outs," eventually gives us inspiration as a working part of the mind.

Self-Nurturing

The Prosperous Heart is self-nurturing. It listens for, and recognizes, its personal needs, wants, and desires. Rather than push forward in a harsh and driven manner, it asks instead what it can do right now to feel at peace. The answers do come, and as the heart learns that it will be listened to, it speaks more gently and specifically. "Your need is rest and water," it may say. Or, "Relax, let go, remember Spirit is in charge."

APRIL 8

The Light at the End of the Tunnel

Money madness breeds despair. We feel we will never get ahead. Solvency breeds hope. We see the light at the end of the tunnel. Our dignity returns.

Abstinence

One of the first fruits of abstinence is increased clarity. We know precisely how much money we have, and we become alert for windfalls. Unexpected money in can be assigned a threefold path: one-third toward debt repayment, one-third toward the present, and one-third in savings toward the future. This formula, practiced by Debtors Anonymous, yields a sense of grounded abundance.

APRIL 10

Our Own Sphere

Too often, we are so focused on the woes of the big picture that we fail to see the good we can do in our own sphere. Acting with generosity and kindness, we have a benevolent impact on all we encounter.

Sharing Knowledge

Often, we have in our acquaintance young people who can benefit from our shared skills. A lesson in cookie baking yields a rich future, as cookies can be gifts for many occasions. A lesson in collage can yield a dividend of increased self-knowledge, as collage is a tool for self-awareness. Help with a résumé, a query letter, or a grant application is help indeed. The skills we pass on may in turn be passed on. Our gifts are valuable.

April 12

Our Dreams

Committed to solvency, we find there is one power flowing through all of life. That power is Spirit. Spirit dreams through us. Our dreams are fulfilled by Spirit.

APRIL 13

Fear

Our dollar bill has emblazoned on it "In God We Trust." Yet most of us trust not in God but in the dollar itself. Money, we are taught, is a buffer against fear. If we have "enough" money, we will feel safe. But there is no such thing as "enough" money. As our assets increase, very often so does our fear of losing them. Instead of believing we will be taken care of, we believe we need to take care.

April 14

Unexpected Expenses

Using Counting as the bedrock tool of fiscal responsibility, we sketch out a Prosperity Plan mapping where
we would like our monies to go. For many of us, this
is the first time we have had a savings account, a con-
tingency fund for unexpected expenses. It's also the
first time we have had an accurate sense of what monies we have and what monies we may use in an emergency.

April 15

Divine Order

Committed to our tools of solvency, we are given the grace of acceptance. Everything is in divine order. We no longer fight Spirit's timing. We come to believe life is unfolding exactly as it should.

APRIL 16

Saving Money

For many of us, "putting something away for a rainy day" is a foreign concept. We are accustomed to spending every nickel we have—and some of us are accustomed to spending more than that. We have a habit of debting, not saving. A tenth of our income allotted to savings is enough to quickly accumulate a buffer against hard times. And when we receive an unexpected windfall, increase the amount allotted to savings to one-third. The remaining two-thirds can be allotted one-third toward debt repayment and one-third toward the present.

April 17

A True Note

Spirit speaks to me and through me. As I listen for guidance, I am given a voice to celebrate what I find. My insights and perceptions are powerful and unique. My voice strikes a true note in the symphony of life.

One Day at a Time

Just as a life without alcohol seems an impossibility to an alcoholic but can be accomplished one day at a time, so, too, a life without debt can be ours in twenty-four-hour increments. "Just for today, I won't debt."

Prospering All

Spirit is a vibrant and dynamic energy. Loving toward all, it prospers with peaceful expansion. As we align ourselves with Spirit, we, too, are prospered. There is enough for all.

April 20

Peace

Sourced in Spirit, I prosper without competition. Solvent, I am led, a step at a time, to a more abundant life. Counting my blessings, I abandon all hostility and aggression. Instead, I walk in peace.

APRIL 21

Faulty Dependency

Recovering from money madness, we recover from faulty dependency. Instead of placing our faith in people, we turn to Spirit as we learn that recovery means reliance on Spirit, not defiance.

APRIL 22

Daring to Dream

The Prosperous Heart is expansive. Freed from the anxiety produced by debting, it holds an abundance of productive, usable energy. Freed from the nightmare of fiscal anxiety, the Prosperous Heart dares to dream.

APRIL 23

Spirit's Help

Spirit unravels our tangled affairs. No situation is too complex or difficult for Spirit to solve. It is Spirit's pleasure to give us aid. When we receive help, we give thanks, and our gratitude overflows.

April 24

Spontaneity

Money mad, we are braced for the worst. Frozen with fear, we dread what we will encounter. Solvent, we find the world friendlier. No longer defensive, we trust our spontaneity.

APRIL 25

Receiving

As we become solvent, abundance comes to us from many sources. In order to receive it, we must practice being openhearted as well as open-minded. Our higher power likes to give. It's our job to receive.

APRIL 26

A Faithful Guide

As we learn to place our affairs in the hands of a higher power, we see results. We are led carefully and well. Gradually we come to realize that we have a faithful guide, an inner prompting that leads us in appropriate directions.

APRIL 27

Small Luxuries

As we sketch out our Prosperity Plan, we allot categories for improved self-care. We find room for small
luxuries. We may buy "good" shampoo or a bar of
scented soap. We may subscribe to a magazine, taking
advantage of a bargain price rather than paying far
more at the newsstand. Making a list of luxury items,
we may find we can afford some of them. A little luxury goes a long way.

April 28

Protected by Spirit

Spirit is within us at the very core of our being. Protected by this inner source, we move through the world with confidence. There is one power. That power is the Spirit within, which guides us to safety and security. As we are sourced in Spirit, no harm comes our way. Spirit sees adversity as opportunity.

Divine Ideas

The Prosperous Heart is grounded in divinity. It knows Spirit is its source. Out of this limitless supply, we think with clarity and ease. Asking for guidance, we are led to divine ideas that are vibrant, dynamic, and original.

APRIL 30

Freedom

The Prosperous Heart is free. Relying upon a higher power, it has unlimited resources. Free to act as it chooses, it listens to the still, small voice, which urges it, always, to expand and prosper. Partnered by Spirit, all things are possible.

May

MAY 1

Faith over Fear

Each of us can make a conscious choice to choose faith over fear. As we place our lives in the hands of a higher power, we consciously choose to be right-sized. Electing humility rather than arrogance, we turn to the Spirit within for guidance at all times.

MAY 2

Self-Love

As we learn to husband our resources, living within our means, we treat ourselves with greater care. We value ourselves more highly and become, in effect, protective parents to ourselves. We learn to use this mantra: Treating myself like a precious object will make me strong.

MAY 3

The Surefooted Guide

As we turn to Spirit for help with our financial affairs, we find the still, small voice amplified. Our inner wisdom becomes the sure-footed guide we follow a step at a time.

MAY 4

Drama

The addiction to financial mismanagement is actually an addiction to drama. Our adrenaline runs high as our self-worth runs low. Shattering our denial, we are after the serenity that solvency brings.

MAY 5

Clearing Clutter

As we hang on to junk, we hang on to shabby self-worth. If we clear away the old, we make way for the new. Clearing clutter literally clears the way to inspiration. Our thinking lightens as a conscious contact with a power greater than ourselves is reinforced.

MAY 6

The Breath of Spirit

We are, each of us, a conduit for the breath of Spirit. Spirit moves through each of us in a unique and indispensable way. As we follow our guidance, we become more truly ourselves. Spirit flows through us, shaped by each of us as light through a crystal prism.

Discernment

When we mismanage our money, we often find ourselves feeling foolish. We are ashamed by our lack of
control. When we commit ourselves to solvency, we
experience self-worth. As we ask to be led, we are led.
As we ask for wisdom, we find ourselves being wise.
We are given the gift of discernment.

MAY 8

Becoming Positive

As we pray for guidance in our financial affairs, we are led to make discerning choices. We no longer experience the world as a hostile place. Instead of hostility and stress, we experience a world of love. As we become more positive, our world becomes positive. We experience Spirit as "good, orderly direction."

MAY 9

Loving Others

The Prosperous Heart is loving. When we place our faith in Spirit as our source, we are freed to love others without neediness. As we recognize that our good comes to us from many directions, we release others from self-centered agendas.

MAY 10

Always the Same

When we are mired in money madness, we are mired in despair. Although our denial tells us each time will be different, in our hearts we know that each failure to manage our money is the same.

MAY 11

Love without Strings

Led by Spirit, we love others with an open hand. We place our dependency on Spirit, not on human resources. As a result of our loving others freely, they, too, can freely love us in return.

MAY 12

Our Considerable Power

When we live within our means, we experience our considerable power. Instead of the darkness of debt, we share the light of solvency. As our fiscal affairs become Spirit's business, not merely our own, we experience solutions in place of problems.

MAY 13

My Unique Destiny

As I turn within, seeking divine guidance, I am led a step at a time to my unique destiny. As I listen for cues, both within me and without, I find that Spirit illuminates my path.

MAY 14

Hardship

Many of us fear a debt-free life. We fear a life of hardship. Yet it is debt that causes hardship. The stress and anxiety of fiscal unmanageability batter our psyches, causing us to live in fear. As we take steps toward solvency, placing our finances in Spirit's hands, we find unexpected comfort.

MAY 15

Sharing Our Good

When we recognize Spirit as our source, good flows to us. We come to experience our life as a river of goodness. Abundance flows to us and through us to others. Tapped into infinite resources, we are able to share our good.

MAY 16

Enough for All

Ours is a rich and plentiful world. There is enough for all of us. When we focus on what we have, we seem to have more. Counting our blessings gives us a sense of abundance.

MAY 17

A Lightness of Heart

When our relationship to money is toxic, we experience the world as a dark and hostile place. Debting causes us to feel grim. We experience a spiral of shame and despair. When we commit our finances to the care of the higher power, we experience an unexpected lightness of heart. The world is no longer dark and threatening. Instead of hardship, we experience grace. Humor lights the world.

MAY 18

The Gift of Enthusiasm

The Prosperous Heart has the gift of enthusiasm. Sourced in Spirit, experienced in grace, we expect to prosper. Our life becomes an adventure. Wonderful things come to us and through us.

MAY 19

Pleasure

As solvency transforms our world, we are freed to experience pleasure. As stress and anxiety vanish, delight and adventure take their place. As we count our blessings, we feel an increased sense of safety and security. We experience serenity.

MAY 20

A Transformed World

Money mad, we are stuck in negativity. We are apprehensive about what our futures may hold. Solvent, we no longer live in dread. We become a conduit for good. Our world is transformed.

MAY 21

Harmony

Committed to live debt-free one day at a time, we experience the melody of a life lived in harmony with our peers. There are no discordant demands. Instead, we are led forward one step at a time.

May 22

The Great Creator

We often call Spirit the "Great Creator" without realizing that *creator* is another term for "artist." We are the Creator's creations, and we are, in turn, intended to be creative ourselves. Creativity is Spirit's gift to us. Using our creativity is a gift back to Spirit.

MAY 23

Alert to Abundance

Blessings build upon blessings. As we focus on what we have rather than what we lack, our blessings increase. Prosperity comes to us in many forms. As we count our blessings, we become alert to abundance.

MAY 24

Compassion

When our finances are out of control, we experience the world as a hostile place. We live lives of anxiety, depression, and despair. Those to whom we owe money are our enemies. The request for payment we experience as harassment. We are without compassion. One of the first fruits of solvency is compassion for others. No longer viewed as enemies, their needs, wants, and desires strike us now as human. We experience the relief of compassion, both for them and for ourselves.

MAY 25

A Divine Energy

When we turn to Spirit for help with our finances, we soon find we have tapped a divine energy. Spirit is wise, good, vibrant, and expansive. So, too, are we, as we trust Spirit to manage our affairs.

MAY 26

Binge Spending

To recover from money madness, many of us must recover from binge spending. Binge spending is often overspending. We indulge ourselves into debt. Solvent, we spend in a timely fashion and within our means.

Having Enough

Debt is born from fear: fear that we will not have enough. Counting on ourselves alone, we steal from our fellows, robbing them of their security, violating their trust. When we place our worldly affairs in the hands of Spirit, we are led and guided one step at a time, much as a loving parent guides a toddler. Soon we begin to have the novel experience of feeling ourselves to be children of the divine.

MAY 28

New Purpose

When we commit ourselves to a life of solvency, we find that our lives take on new purpose and meaning. Freed from anxiety, freed from stress, we find we have optimism. Safe in Spirit's keeping, we dare to dream. Touched by grace, our dreams have higher goals.

MAY 29

The Symphony of Life

Sourced in Spirit, each of us becomes a unique and original individual. No two souls are alike. Each sounds a pure and true note in the symphony of life. We are all part of Spirit's harmony.

Hope

When we allow money to be our master, we frequently feel despair. We never have "enough" to give us security. We are always wanting more. When money becomes our servant, we experience hope. Sourced in Spirit, we are optimistic, hopeful of a future filled with blessings.

MAY 31

Adversity

In our financial recovery, we are given what we need.
Spirit sees adversity as opportunity. One door closes
and another opens. We are led to prosperity a step at a
time.

June

JUNE 1

Redemption

Spirit created the world. Spirit sees all and knows all. There is no situation too tangled or complex for Spirit's redeeming touch. As we seek spiritual help in our worldly affairs, we experience redemption. No longer alone or lonely, we have the companionship of Spirit to see us through.

JUNE 2

Happiness

Happiness is a by-product of right action. It is not an end in itself. When we seek to know and do the will of Spirit, we experience joy. We seek serenity and we find peace. Gradually, our happiness becomes a habitual state.

JUNE 3

Service

When we seek to do Spirit's will, we are often called to do service. Seeking to serve others, we find ourselves. Self-centered agendas fade away. Released from the bondage of self, we experience generosity.

JUNE 4

Blessings

Money mad, we often blame Spirit for our lives of duress. Solvent, we begin to practice gratitude, counting our blessings, seeing the glass half full, not half empty. As we practice gratitude, our blessings multiply. Our lives become rich. We thank Spirit for the many gifts bestowed.

JUNE 5

Serenity

The Prosperous Heart is serene. Secure in the knowledge that Spirit guides and guards our affairs, we experience peace. We are safe and secure. There are no emergencies.

A Return to Sanity

Money mad, with our money unmanageable, we feel crazy. We spiral into shame and self-loathing. When we begin the work toward solvency, we begin to feel sane and serene. Solvency is a return to sanity.

JUNE 7

Willingness

As we place our lives in the hands of Spirit, we experience the willingness to accept a higher hand working
in our affairs. As we open our minds and our hearts to
Spirit's promptings, we experience solutions in the
place of problems.

JUNE 8

Shattering Denial

Counting is a simple tool, yet a profound one. As we set down our expenditures, money in, money out, in black and white, we find ourselves shattering our denial. Self-knowledge replaces vagueness.

JUNE 9

Being Lighthearted

Focused lightly on the natural world—the moon's gentle phases, the cloud sailing serenely across the sky—we begin to sense that the Great Creator is playful. We, too, can tread more lightly, taking delight in the world as we find it, focusing on the positive, not the negative.

June 10

Courage

Committed to solvency, we experience courage. Spirit is our protector and our guide. Believing in "good, orderly direction"—God—we face obstacles with equanimity. Brave enough to face our finances honestly, we are given the gift of courage.

JUNE 11

Simplicity

Belief means reliance, not defiance. It is really very simple: Spirit is the source of our good. The tools of solvency are simple tools. As we practice them, we become both humble and authentic.

June 12

Solutions

To Spirit, our adversity is an opportunity to help. It is Spirit's nature to give and it is our job to receive. As we take our problems to Spirit, we find solutions. Guarded and guided, we experience ourselves as children of the divine.

JUNE 13

A New Serenity

For many of us, the end of money madness is the end of erraticism. No longer addicted to drama and adrenaline, we find our lives have a new consistency and serenity.

Valuable Gifts

Each of us is an important part of the whole. As we share with others our solvency, we mentor them by example. There is abundance enough for all of us, and our faith in the generosity of the Universe is contagious.

JUNE 15

The Divine Mind

As I turn to Spirit as the source of my good, I am divinely led. My good comes to me from all directions, from people and events. I am alert to guidance in its many forms, both within me and from the world. Spirit knows the answers to my problems and questions. As I open my mind to Spirit's influx, I experience a wisdom greater than my own. The divine mind thinks through me. I think through the divine mind.

June 16

Goodness

The Prosperous Heart is charitable, generous in its dealings with others. It offers heartfelt and genuine support. Spirit is love, and that divine love moves us to act in benevolent ways. As we take small, positive actions, we change our world for the better.

JUNE 17

Expanding Our Good

Too often, we feel small and ineffectual. We wonder, what can one person do to impact our troubled world? With Spirit acting through us, we can do a great deal. When we seek to do Spirit's will, we find our good expanding.

JUNE 18

Imagination

Spirit gifts us with imagination. Many of us abuse this gift, practicing pessimism and calling it realism. When we consciously choose to imagine events unfolding in a benevolent and optimistic way, then we are using our imaginations rightly. As we visualize an optimistic future, we practice a form of affirmative prayer.

JUNE 19

Grace

Sourced in Spirit, we feel compassion for others, acting toward them with authentic kindness. Spirit tutors us in generosity. As we open our hearts, we are led to charity. We are within Spirit and Spirit is within us. Divine intelligence acts in our affairs. Divine grace blesses those we encounter.

JUNE 20

Easy Does It

The recovery from money madness is a recovery from urgency and a misplaced sense of emergency. Detoxing from our adrenaline-fueled lives, we begin to practice a new slogan: Easy does it.

JUNE 21

Identity

Too often, we seek to forge an identity based on our worldly successes. We are what we do and what we've done. We identify ourselves with our careers. Sourced in Spirit, we soon take a different view of such short-sightedness. We are children of the divine, we realize. We are worthy of love and respect apart from our jobs. As we seek to know and do Spirit's will, we find ourselves rewarded by genuine self-esteem.

June 22

Connection

Rooted in our solvency, we find ourselves less dependent upon our fellows. As we become more authentically ourselves, we are able to encounter those we meet without neediness. We are able to release others from our agendas, loving others truly as they wish to be loved.

JUNE 23

Authenticity

The Prosperous Heart is authentic. Its dreams and goals are grounded in personal values. Seeking to be true to ourselves, we are able to relate more honestly to others. Becoming solvent, we meet our truth and ourselves.

JUNE 24

Becoming Right-Sized

Sourced in Spirit, we become right-sized. We respond humbly and without false pride to the demands of the world. Blessed with grace, we are able to meet obstacles with honesty. Freed from grandiose expectations, we seek the silver lining in all our affairs.

Expectation

The Prosperous Heart counts its many blessings. It practices the mantra, "My life is a treasure." Counting its blessings, it finds good. It expects to prosper, and it does.

JUNE 26

Our Unique Destiny

Every soul has a unique path. As we commit ourselves to Spirit, that path is revealed to us. We are led well and carefully, a step at a time. As we follow our guidance, we are moved to put our faith into action. As we listen to our cues both internally and externally, our life becomes unique and adventuresome. Wonderful things come to pass for us and others.

JUNE 27

Harvest

As we commit ourselves to Spirit, we commit ourselves to trusting Spirit's higher wisdom. Rooted in our solvency, we anticipate a beautiful harvest as being natural and expected. Today's dreams become tomorrow's realities. Spirit's harvest is rich and abundant.

JUNE 28

An End to Loneliness

The energy, power, and love of Spirit runs through all of life. As we commit ourselves to solvency, we find ourselves united with all. No longer plagued by loneliness and anxious apartness, we are connected in Spirit to a vast family.

JUNE 29

This Beautiful World

Spirit is within me and I am within Spirit. As I look
with Spirit's eyes, I see the beauty that surrounds me: a
crystal prism, a radiant lily, a delicate fern. As I appreciate Spirit's artistry, I come, too, to appreciate myself.
Appreciating all, I prosper.

June 30

Change for the Better

Money mad, we are on a treadmill. Our lives are filled with apprehension and dread. Each day feels the same. Solvent, our lives become rich and variable. We embrace change, knowing that it is change for the better.

July

JULY 1

A Larger Plan

Each of us is a unique gateway for Spirit's good to enter the world. As we open our minds and hearts, Spirit's wisdom and power pour through us. As we cooperate with Spirit in our unfolding, we are a part of a larger plan.

July 2

Spirit's Impact

The Prosperous Heart draws comfort from its connection to Spirit. No longer anxious and overwhelmed, it finds itself safe and secure. The power of Spirit is its protection. The guidance of Spirit is its security. In Spirit's care, we are safe.

JULY 3

Peace

Counting my blessings, I walk in peace. Spirit's abundance gives me a broad and gentle path. As I trust Spirit, I myself am trustworthy. As Spirit harmonizes all, I walk in the world without enmity.

JULY 4

An Inner Compass

All of us contain an inner compass. Its needle points us home toward our true values. When we pay attention to our inner compass, we find ourselves doing "the next right thing." If our small steps are attuned to our values, then we will find ourselves enacting Spirit's will in the larger picture. Very often, the next right thing is something small. Fifteen minutes of clearing clutter, fifteen minutes spent sorting our mail—these small acts make up the larger movements of our life.

JULY 5

Never Alone

Spirit knows no distance. I am always held safe and secure in the very heart of divine love. As I work toward solvency, I am never alone, never without divine companionship.

Effortless Love

Divine love loves through me. Sourced in Spirit, I extend myself without strain or exertion. Rather, my love is effortless. Spirit is expansive, and I expand through Spirit.

JULY 7

One Life

Spirit is the source of all life. As I turn to Spirit for strength and guidance, I feel my connection to all of life. The oak, the rose, the deer, the squirrel—one life runs through all. I am connected to all living things.

July 8

Spiritual Help

The Prosperous Heart is never without spiritual help. As it seeks guidance and protection, it has a divine companion. Guided and guarded, there is no error in its path. Led to solvency, it finds serenity.

JULY 9

Divine Abundance

When I turn within, seeking a contact with Spirit, I am gifted with eyes that see the beauty all around me. This world is beautiful and prosperous, reflecting the beauty of its creator. I, too, am meant to prosper. Although I seldom see it, I, too, am made in the Creator's image. Seeking solvency, I encounter divine abundance.

A Free Heart

When our finances are tangled, we experience our lives as tangled. When our finances are serene, we experience joy. Placing our affairs in the hands of Spirit, our hearts are freed from worry and anxiety.

A Day at a Time

When we live without debting, we find ourselves well and carefully led. Our graceful good comes to us through our commitment to Spirit. As we ask for guidance, we receive it. The prompting of Spirit comes to us both internally and in the world around us. We know intuitively how to handle situations. Grace gives us the courage not to debt a day at a time.

July 12

Benefits of Solvency

Using our Counting to tabulate money in and money out, we build a Prosperity Plan. As we get in touch with our true values, we begin to welcome new and right activities and people into our lives. We spend our time and money more wisely.

JULY 13

My True Self

As I commit myself to Spirit, I commit myself to being truly myself. Mentored by Spirit, I find my true path. I am original—that is, I am the origin of my world.

July 14

A Generous Citizen

Freed from my anxiety about money, I find myself openhearted. No longer constricted by fear, I experience myself as a generous citizen of the world. Listening for promptings both within and without, I have a sense of safety and expansion. As I open my heart to Spirit, I am led.

An Inner Guide

Freed from the turbulence of debt, sourced in Spirit, I encounter an inner guide. I am wiser than I have often known. Following my guidance, I find a sure path.

JULY 16

Trustworthy

As we live within our means, we become trustworthy. We no longer debt, borrowing against our future and abusing those to whom we owe money. Sourced in Spirit, we become wise. We are stronger and more resilient as we turn within for Spirit's counsel. We are good. We are reliable. We can be trusted.

JULY 17

Spiritual Protection

As we turn to Spirit, invoking divine guidance and assistance, we find ourselves the recipients of spiritual
protection. Sourced in Spirit, trusting that Spirit guides
and guards us and our affairs, we find a sense of safety
and security. With Spirit at the center of our lives, no
harm comes to us.

JULY 18

Spirit's Power

As we ask to be relieved of the bondage of self, we turn to Spirit and experience freedom. Spirit's power becomes our power. No longer limited by our human fears, we are freed to expand with divine protection.

Conscious Choice

As we change our thinking, we change our world. As I choose to invoke divine help in my financial affairs, I find myself making many a conscious choice that moves me from pessimism to optimism. I am vigilant to discard all negativity. My word is positive and powerful.

JULY 20

Our Value

When our money is manageable, we have clarity. Our unique selves shine. Spirit cherishes us. We are jewels in the crown of Spirit—rubies, diamonds, emeralds, and more. We are valuable.

JULY 21

Safety

Prosperity isn't about money. It is about the sense of safety that comes to us from knowing we are well cared for. Prosperity is a matter of faith. When we believe in a benevolent Universe, one that looks out for our needs and wants, we feel prosperous.

What Is Enough?

When we say we have enough—always enough—what do we mean by that? Put simply, we mean that we acknowledge Spirit as our source. We are safe and secure, held in Spirit's loving hands, protected from all harm, guided and guarded at all times. We have a sense of prosperity, a belief in an abundant Universe. We acknowledge our source as spiritual rather than fiscal. Like the child who gave Jesus the loaves and fishes, we give our meager supplies over to Spirit that they may be multiplied and enlarged.

JULY 23

Trust

Many of us have been raised to trust the power of the dollar, even though our dollars declare, "In God We Trust." The truth is, in God we don't trust. We need to learn that we live in a benevolent Universe. There is a divine source always on the lookout for our well-being. To that force, difficulties are always opportunities. Each hardship is a chance to grow spiritually.

JULY 24

New Energy

A recovery from money madness is often the cue for creativity. Our energies are freed from chronic acting out. This influx of new energy brings with it new, vibrant, and vital ideas.

July 25

Wise Choices

When we place our financial affairs in the hands of Spirit, we experience calm. We find ourselves in touch with an inner wisdom. We are clear about our priorities. Freed from anxiety, depression, and a sense of emergency, we make wise choices.

JULY 26

No Longer Frightened

When our money is out of control, we experience the world as a hostile place. We are afraid to open our mail. We are afraid to answer our telephone. Anything that looks official or financial frightens us. We are anxious, even panicked. What a change it is when we become solvent, placing our finances in the hands of Spirit. No longer frightened, we experience a benevolent world.

No Longer the Enemy

When our money is out of control, we experience others as the enemy. Our debts are demands. We often blame others for our unmanageability. When we become solvent, we are able to view others with compassion and love. They are no longer the enemy.

The Divine Spark

Solvent, we become clear. To others, we are often a fountain of light. Peace, prosperity, and power flow through us. We are a conduit for divinity. As we express the divine spark within us, grace flows through our lives, touching all we encounter.

Self-Worth

Living beyond our means, we experience the thorn of anxiety. It pierces our composure and sense of well-being. Living within our means, we experience comfort. There are no rude shocks or abusive phone calls. We have self-worth.

July 30

Anchored

Counting, we experience an inner calm. Even in times of turbulence, we are anchored. We feel ourselves safe and companioned. We are carried forward by grace. Counting, we are led. Spirit anchors us.

JULY 31

Laughter

When we are debting, our world is dark and humorless. We have a sense of anxiety and emergency. Our finances are no laughing matter. Abstinent, we experience lightness of heart. The world is filled with blessings, among them good humor. Laughter blesses our path.

August

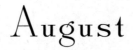

AUGUST 1

Filled with God

The word *enthusiasm* comes from the Greek, meaning "filled with God." The Prosperous Heart is enthusiastic. It expects to prosper. Its life is an adventure. It sees good in every direction it looks.

August 2

Attuned to Spirit

Spirit is an expansive energy. As we attune ourselves to Spirit, we, too, expand. Spirit is harmonious. Attuned to Spirit, we are in harmony with those around us.

August 3

Intending Good

Life is intentional, not accidental. Our choices reflect our values. Our values reflect purpose and meaning. As we intend good, we are led to greater goodness.

August 4

Secrecy

For many of us, money is a loaded subject. Frequently, we experience discussion of money as taboo. Our shame around money leads us to secrecy. Our secrecy, in turn, leads us to shame.

August 5

Spirit's Inflow

Just as blood is part of our physical body, creativity is part of our spiritual body. All souls are creative. As we open our minds and hearts to the Great Creator, we experience an inflow of originality and vitality.

AUGUST 6

Small Changes

Money mad, we indulge in drama. We daydream of a grand windfall that will clear our debts in one fell swoop. Solvent, we learn to appreciate small changes. Each tiny step for the better increases our self-worth.

August 7

Blessings Multiply

The Prosperous Heart counts its many blessings. Focused on the positive, it finds that its blessings multiply. Blessings come in many forms, through people and events. Blessings may be both large and small. Grounded in gratitude, we have a feeling of abundance.

AUGUST 8

Compassion

The Prosperous Heart feels compassion for others and itself. It has tenderness toward human fears. Protected and led, we can protect and lead others.

AUGUST 9

Carefully Led

Solvent, we experience grace—a flow of unwarranted good working in our best interest. We are dowried by Spirit with the gifts of composure, wisdom, and discernment. Our paths become smooth. We are carefully led.

August 10

A Child of the Divine

Ours is an abundant Universe. Its blessings come in many forms. The Prosperous Heart sources itself in Spirit, and as it does so, it prospers. Solvent, it lays claim to being a child of the divine.

Charity

The Prosperous Heart is charitable. Sourced in Spirit, it is sourced in love. Counting its blessings, it feels abundance. Confident that it is safe and secure, it extends itself in generosity toward others less fortunate.

AUGUST 12

Freed from Bondage

Freed from the bondage of shortsighted and self-centered goals, generous rather than stingy, the Prosperous Heart serves others as well as itself.

AUGUST 13

Postponing Our Dreams

Money mad, we often postpone our dreams until we have "enough" money. Solvent, we no longer procrastinate. We pursue our dreams a step at a time.

August 14

Looking Ahead

Grounded by its connection to Spirit, the Prosperous
Heart has no fear of the future. Rather than looking
ahead with dread, it looks ahead with confidence. Our
Money Map tells us where our money goes currently.
Our Prosperity Plan channels our flow along ever-
better lines. Our money is our servant, not our master.

Our True Nature

Spirit is within all of us. Majestic yet tender, it is the divine spark that animates us all. We are children of the divine. Revealed to us through solvency, our true nature is spiritual.

Finding Ourselves

It takes courage to commit to Spirit. Our human fear is that we will lose ourselves. The opposite is true. As we commit to Spirit, we become more truly ourselves.

AUGUST 17

Transformation

Financial mismanagement creates isolation. Isolation creates loneliness. As we turn to Spirit for help with our finances, we unexpectedly experience a sense of divine companionship. Our loneliness ebbs away as serenity and contentment take its place.

August 18

Authentic Connection

As we commit ourselves to Spirit, we are freed from faulty dependencies. Rather than forge friendships grounded in neediness, we instead place our reliance upon Spirit, freeing ourselves to encounter others authentically.

Freedom Accounts

Money mad, we live beyond our means. The more we make, the more we spend. Solvent, we channel our excess funds into savings, or "freedom accounts." Our spending becomes rational, not impulsive.

August 20

Loving the World

Life is intended to be sweet and cherished. This world is beautiful. We are intended to love its many delights. As we love the world, we love Spirit, its creator. As we love Spirit, we love the world.

Spirit's Delight

There is one life animating all of creation. That light is Spirit, which takes delight in expressing itself in many forms. Our dreams come from our divinity. Spirit longs to express itself through us. Our yearnings come from a divine source, and it gives Spirit pleasure to fulfill them.

The Natural World

Solvent, we lose our defensiveness. The world becomes Spirit's gift to us. Cherishing all that we find—the wild primrose, the butterfly, the hawk—we count the blessings of the natural world and we experience our own natural grace.

AUGUST 23

Divinely Prospered

In Spirit, there is no competition. We are all divinely led and prospered. There is abundance enough for all of us to share. Spirit flows out from us toward all we encounter.

August 24

A Gateway for Blessings

As I commit myself to Spirit, I open my mind and my heart to its inflow. I become a portal for the grace of Spirit to enter the world. I am a gateway for blessings for myself and others.

AUGUST 25

God's Garden

Spirit takes delight in diversity. Grounded in Spirit's soil, we bloom abundantly. We are God's garden and we prosper through his power.

No Longer Jealous

Money mad, we are prone to jealousy. Solvent, we act on our own behalf and move in the direction of our dreams. Our lives become rich and abundant. We are no longer jealous.

AUGUST 27

The Heart of Spirit

There is no distance from the heart of Spirit. We are always in the center of Spirit's love. We are held safe and secure. We are protected and prospered.

AUGUST 28

Attraction

Money madness invites isolation. We feel alone and threatened. Our finances are our secret. As we move toward solvency, we move toward other people. We are now trustworthy, and people are attracted to us as never before. They lend us encouragement and support.

AUGUST 29

The Power of Spirit

Wise and discerning, Spirit is able to prosper our worldly affairs. Solvent, immersed in divine life, we experience abundance. The kingdom of Spirit is always at hand. We experience prosperity and plenty. The power of Spirit becomes our own.

August 30

Spirit as My Mentor

Spirit's power is personal and intimate. As I turn within for guidance, I meet my teacher and my guide. There is nothing too large or too small for Spirit's loving attention. A step at a time, I am led carefully forward. With Spirit as my mentor, there is no error in my path.

AUGUST 31

Prospering All

There is one power, one presence, one life that flows
through all. As we affirm our abundance, we affirm
our connection to that source. We claim for ourselves
prosperity, knowing that Spirit hears and answers our
prayers. We prosper and bring good to all we encounter.

September

SEPTEMBER 1

Listening for Guidance

Many of us pray for guidance and then rush ahead, rather than listen for an answered prayer. Guidance comes from many sources. It may be the hunch, the inspiration, the "funny feeling," the "still, small voice" forming within. It may be the words of a stranger overheard, the synchronicity of events. Guidance comes from within and without. We are led carefully and well. There is no error in our path. We need only listen, realizing that no prayer goes unanswered.

Setting Limits

In recovery from money madness, we learn to practice the new skill of limit setting. We establish a bottom line of behaviors we will no longer indulge in. Setting these limits and sticking to them are important steps toward health.

SEPTEMBER 3

Spirit's Solution

When our money is mismanaged, we feel alone and threatened. When we place our finances in Spirit's hands, we enjoy a sense of connection. There is no problem too grave or too complex for Spirit. Spirit solves all difficulties.

Loyalty

Solvent, feeling protected myself, I am able to extend myself to others. My loyalty is a boon to my relationships. Continuity is a gift I offer those I love.

SEPTEMBER 5

Limitless Strength

When my finances are unstable, I find myself weak and overwhelmed. When my finances are secure in Spirit's hands, I feel my strength. It is abundant. Tapping into Spirit as source, I have limitless strength and resilience.

SEPTEMBER 6

A Kingdom of Joy

Spirit is the great giver. But it cannot give what we will not receive. Too often, we are convinced this world is a veil of tears. Turning to Spirit, we find a world of joy. As we open our minds and hearts to the possibility that the kingdom of Spirit is one of happiness, we find our hearts become joyous. Our lives become buoyant.

September 7

A Brave New Heart

Today and every day I anticipate good. I open my mind and heart to the inflow of Spirit, recognizing the gifts it brings to bear. Grounded in Spirit, I expect and encounter new loves. I open a brave new heart. I prosper.

September 8

An Inflow of Grace

When my money is unmanageable, my life is unmanageable. My energy is closed. My heart is shuttered. When I give my finances to Spirit, I experience an inflow of grace. I am no longer stingy or miserly. Instead, I am openhearted.

SEPTEMBER 9

A Step at a Time

Spirit leads us a step at a time. We are guided carefully and well. There is no error in our path. We move forward in faith, trusting Spirit as a faithful guide.

September 10

Thoughtfulness

As my finances stabilize, guarded and protected by
Spirit, I become trustworthy, no longer erratic or self-
centered. The Prosperous Heart is thoughtful of others.

Comparison

Money madness frequently has its roots in comparison. We judge our insides by someone else's outsides. We always come up short. There will always be those who have "more." Solvent, we know there is enough for all of us.

SEPTEMBER 12

Divine Energy

As we seek to align ourselves with Spirit's will for us, our affairs become fruitful and harmonious. Acting always on our behalf, Spirit pours grace and abundance into our hearts. This divine energy shelters and guides us.

SEPTEMBER 13

Good Health

Money mad, we often neglect our physical selves. We avoid exercise, fearing the feelings it would entail. Solvent, we learn to pursue good health.

Unity as Prosperity

Spirit is transformational. As I commit myself to Spirit, I become a portal for its grace to enter the world. One life runs through all of life. As I experience unity, I find my prosperity.

SEPTEMBER 15

Divine Ideas

Committed to Spirit, we are tapped into a limitless flow of creativity. Divine mind thinks through us. Rather than our finite selves, we experience an infinite flow of divine ideas. We come to rely on this flow, and as we do, we prosper.

September 16

Discernment

When our finances are snarled, we feel threatened and trapped. When we turn over our finances to Spirit, we experience freedom. Sourced in Spirit, we are no longer afraid. Instead, we move forward with confidence, choosing our path with discernment.

SEPTEMBER 17

The Prosperity Plan

Counting is a daily practice. The Money Map is a monthly practice. These tools, in turn, generate a Prosperity Plan. Our Prosperity Plan allows us a conscious choice about into what tributaries our monies will flow.

SEPTEMBER 18

A Turn for the Better

When we are in debt, with our finances veering out of
our control, we experience a frightening world of ani-
mosity. As we are willing to begin a quest for solvency
and turn to Spirit to guide our affairs, we meet a new
and benevolent world.

Staying in the Day

Caught up in money madness, we often visualize a grandiose future. We will be rich, famous, respected. In recovery, our visions of the future become more real. Our dignity does not hinge on the dollar. Staying in the day, we build a prosperous future one step at a time.

SEPTEMBER 20

Love without Strings

When we depend upon Spirit as our source, we are freed from unhealthy dependency on others. Our good flows to us from many directions, freeing us to love others without neediness.

Procrastination in Place of Clarity

Financial mismanagement builds procrastination. We will get to our mail later, we tell ourselves. We will listen to our phone messages later. Frequently we feel harassed by bill collectors. We procrastinate in place of clarity. Taking a small positive action on our own solvent behalf is all it takes to break out of the rut of procrastination. Active, we move toward clarity.

SEPTEMBER 22

A Gentle Path

Sourced in Spirit, we find comfort. We find compassion, kindness, and tenderness. Our path is broad and gentle.

Benevolent Surprises

Money mad, we are always braced apprehensively for life's negative surprises. Solvent, we look forward to life. Its surprises are benevolent.

September 24

Spirit's Harmony

When our finances are in disarray, we experience the world as discordant. When we commit our finances to the hands of Spirit, our relationships grow sweet and tender. We experience harmony.

Opportunity

One spirit, one life, one energy, flows through all of creation. It is a river of goodness that we can tap into as we commit to Spirit. As we seek a silver lining, all adversity becomes opportunity.

September 26

Dishonesty

Money madness is founded on dishonesty. We make ourselves out to be more than what we are. We spend more than what we have. We borrow with little thought of repayment. Solvency is founded on honesty. We live within our means. Honest, we are filled with hope.

Grace

When we align our will with Spirit's will for us, we experience grace. Good flows to us, filling our hearts with compassion, kindness, and tenderness. Once discordant, the world is now harmonious.

September 28

Freed from Anxiety

Financial disarray is no laughing matter. When our finances are troubled, the world seems troubled as well. When we commit our finances to Spirit, we experience relief and a lightness of heart. When we are freed from anxiety, humor lights our path.

Joyous Expectancy

Sourced in Spirit, we experience enthusiasm. We see good in all directions. We expect to prosper and we expect our prosperity to prosper those we meet. We have a joyous expectancy of the future. We know that good will come to pass.

September 30

Money as Power

When we are money mad, the world is a competitive place. We pursue money as power. When we are solvent, the world is friendlier. We no longer pursue money as power. Such an adversarial stance is no longer necessary.

October

October 1

Freed from Fear

When our finances are unwieldy, we find ourselves
tormented by fears. When our finances are placed in
the care of Spirit, we are freed from fear and we experience pleasure. All good things can now come to us.
We are led carefully and well. Joy is our companion.

OCTOBER 2

No Harm

Spirit is a nurturing energy. When we commit to Spirit, we find ourselves nurtured. As we connect to the good within us all, we are protected, that no harm may come to us.

OCTOBER 3

A Treacherous Cycle

For many of us, credit cards spell disaster. We load up one card to its maximum and then move on to another. Credit cards tell us we have more funds at our disposal than we do. We overspend, then look for further credit. It is a treacherous cycle. Solvent, we are free from this treacherous cycle.

OCTOBER 4

A Life of Action

As we commit ourselves to solvency, we commit ourselves to a life of action. We are guided carefully and
well, with knowledge of what step to take next. Spirit
acts through us. Going within, we are tutored in what
to do and how to do it. We are compelled to act on our
own behalf.

OCTOBER 5

Spirit's Guidance

"Spirit, please guide and guard my finances," we pray. We ask for knowledge of Spirit's will for us and the power to carry that out. Our lives are touched by joyous harmony and we experience the flow of Spirit's love.

OCTOBER 6

Breaking Denial

Counting tells us where our money goes. Many of us are vague about our spending. Setting it down in black and white gives us an accurate picture of our behaviors. We often spend more than we make and borrow ahead to cover shortfalls. Counting exposes such behaviors and breaks denial.

OCTOBER 7

A Force for the Good

When we place our financial affairs in Spirit's hands, we become a fountain of light. There is an irresistible force for the good that permeates all our endeavors. We prosper and help others to prosper.

OCTOBER 8

Work We Love

When we are money mad, all that we like about our job is the pay. In solvency, we ask, "What do I love doing?" We can often be paid for work that we love.

Dignity

As we recover from our financial mismanagement, we recover our dignity. As we practice abstinence—no debting—we grow in self-esteem.

OCTOBER 10

Adrenaline

Money mismanagement is a form of addiction. We are habituated to anxiety. Lack of money, or the misuse of funds, fills our life with adrenaline. It often seems impossible to us to practice abstinence. But it is possible, and we can begin to do it a day at a time.

OCTOBER 11

Money as Taboo

For many of us, talking about money is as taboo as talking about sex. We don't want to reveal our shame-laden money secrets. Recovery starts with honesty. As we reveal our secrets to a trusted other, we begin to end the spiral of shame.

OCTOBER 12

Once Again Trustworthy

Fiscal unmanageability destroys sweet relationships. We often borrow from family and friends. We often fail to repay the debts we owe. We chase the "big deal" we hope will clear the slate. When it doesn't, we are often volatile. Solvency brings peace and restored faith. We are once again trustworthy.

Money Martyrs

Some of us are addicted to lack. We underearn and then feel morally superior to those who have money. When we do have cash, we spend it on others rather than ourselves. We overpay our fair share of household expenses. We deprive ourselves and feel virtuous in our deprivation. We are money martyrs.

OCTOBER 14

Cash Codependency

Money is a common arena for codependency. Many of us function as savings and loans for our beloveds. We are afraid to say "no" when asked to bankroll some new scheme. Our money is not our own.

OCTOBER 15

Money as Worth

Our society programs us to find our self-worth in money. Rich equals smart, poor equals dumb. We are what we earn, and what we earn is never enough. Many of us have a "magic number," a figure that we tell ourselves will solve all of our problems, yielding us a life of happiness. The problem with the magic number is that it always goes up. When we let go of money as the measure of our worth, we are free to discover our true worth.

OCTOBER 16

Self-Loathing

The addiction to acting out with money becomes a repetitive cycle. We promise ourselves to be better, but we cannot keep our promises. Instead, we debt again and spiral into shame. Self-loathing is the result. Working one day at a time with our solvency tools, our self-loathing slips away.

OCTOBER 17

Passion

Money madness dulls our perceptions. We inhabit a
distorted world. Solvent, we gain clarity. The world
becomes a hospitable place. Our passions return to us.
We dare to dream.

OCTOBER 18

Terminal Vagueness

Many of us practice denial when it comes to our finances. We are vague about what we earn and what we spend. This terminal vagueness allows us to continue our fiscal unmanageability. We know we're in trouble, but we deny ourselves the right to know how much trouble. Counting, we give ourselves the gift of clarity.

OCTOBER 19

Debt Repayment

As we work to become solvent, it is important not only that we put an end to debt, but also that we repay the debts from our past. We need to set a plan for repayment in motion. Debt repayment should be gradual. We must not promise to pay more than we can. Living within our means, and repaying our debts in dollar amounts that are manageable for us, we are filled with hope.

October 20

Discussing Money

For many of us, discussing money is a volatile topic. This is where Counting stands us in good stead. We know what we have spent and how. As we learn to tally our daily Counting into our monthly Money Map, we are able to face a discussion without shame or defensiveness.

Living in the Present

Solvency focuses our attention on the present. We learn we must care for ourselves well now, rather than wait, pie-in-the-sky, for some future windfall. For example, many of us have no allotment for entertainment. Yet a life without fun is unlivable, and we may debt in revenge. Allowing ourselves a budget for that which delights us, we stay naturally—happily—in the present.

OCTOBER 22

Objectivity

Counting is a tool of objectivity, not negativity. It allows us to focus on our money without condemnation. As we tally our weekly Counting into a monthly Money Map, we see areas where we mis-spend. This allows us to make adjustments. Money becomes our friend.

The Bottom Line

Often as we seek to establish solvency, we face waves of anger: our own and from those around us. As we shatter denial, we establish for ourselves a financial bottom line, behaviors we will no longer indulge in or tolerate. As we set these new boundaries, anger is often a side effect.

OCTOBER 24

Toxic Behaviors

Admitting that our lives are financially unmanageable is the first step toward solvency. As we set a bottom line of toxic behaviors, we often find ourselves facing how far we've gone astray. This clarity allows us to change.

The Hope of Health

As we commit to solvency, we commit to the hope of healthy finances. As we shatter our denial and set a bottom line, we begin to move, one day at a time, one dollar at a time, in the direction of health.

OCTOBER 26

An End to Isolation

Financial unmanageability drives us into isolation. We avoid our mail, we avoid our phone, we avoid social situations that we would enjoy. Solvency is a return to normality. We cease isolating as we rejoin society.

Faith Replaces Dread

When we let go of money madness and embrace solvency, we let go of fear. Faith replaces dread as new
behaviors replace the old.

OCTOBER 28

Chronic Spending

Some of us are chronic spenders. We earn enough but overspend. Our bucket has a hole in it. Whenever we have money, we feel compelled to run through it. Solvent, we can learn to build our savings, "spending" our money on our future.

OCTOBER 29

Money as Neutral

Until we achieve solvency and stability, we may be addicted to the mood-altering quality of money. Money mad, our finances make us feel wonderful or horrible. It is never neutral. Solvent, money is drained of its charge. We experience the serenity of neutrality.

OCTOBER 30

Fiscal Grandiosity

Money mad, with our finances out of control, our spending takes on a competitive quality as we compare ourselves to others and come up short. We never have "enough." We always want more. We never feel sufficient without fiscal grandiosity. The newest car, designer clothes, a swanky address. We try to buy our self-worth with all of these, often driving ourselves further into debt.

OCTOBER 31

Money Misers

When we are money misers, addicted to underearning and the anxiety of living by our wits, we are often afraid to ask for money. We "should" have enough, we tell ourselves, without what we see as the shame-filled humiliation of asking for a fair wage. Money misers are just as sick as chronic spenders.

November

NOVEMBER 1

A Learned Skill

Often we assume that being "good" with money is a
knack, not a skill. The truth is, the tools of money
management are simple and easy to learn. As hard as it
is to believe, anyone who is willing to work with the
tools can indeed become good with money.

November 2

Driven to Debt

Money madness is a disease of obsession. We "have" to spend because we "have" to possess a certain object, no matter that we've done well without it. The obsession tells us we must make a purchase. It drives us into debt we claim is justified.

NOVEMBER 3

A Self-Fulfilling Prophecy

Money madness is a self-fulfilling prophecy. Feeling like a failure, we often act like one. Troubled by our debts, we often play credit card roulette, debting further. Changing our behaviors a step at a time, we are led out of debt and into solvency.

November 4

Learning New Tools

When our money is unmanageable, many of us experience a deep-seated sense of shame. We are stupid, bad
people, we tell ourselves. But this is not the case. When
we place our money in the hands of Spirit, we experience growing self-worth. We are willing to learn new
tools, and these tools bring us new freedom.

NOVEMBER 5

Toxic Patterns

Many of us have finances that spiral out of control. Our denial tells us each time that this time will be different. We are victims of our own wrong thinking. "Terminal vagueness," we call it. Denial condemns us to repeating toxic patterns. Counting breaks our denial, freeing us from our toxic patterns.

November 6

"This Time Will Be Different . . ."

We don't want to believe that we are liars, yet many of us have made empty promises to reform our spending. We pledge that we will repay our debts, even as our behaviors are creating new ones. "This time will be different," we tell ourselves and others. But until we surrender to spiritual help, our toxic patterns repeat.

NOVEMBER 7

Reaching the Bottom

For many of us, our financial woes rob us of our integrity. "I have to change," we tell ourselves each time we hit a new financial bottom. It is only when we admit "I cannot change" that our bottom brings recovery. Admitting our need for spiritual help, we pray that our bottom has finally been reached.

Our True Needs

Money madness tempts us to debt for many things we don't really need. Solvency shows us our true needs. We learn to distinguish desires from necessities.

NOVEMBER 9

Tools for Clarity

Using our financial tools—Counting, the Money Map, the Prosperity Plan—we emerge from terminal vagueness into clarity. Often for the first time, we know what we have and how we spend it. We tally our weekly Counting into a monthly Money Map. Using this map, we construct a Prosperity Plan. Our money is like a river with many tributaries. We can adjust the flow to go where it is needed.

Courage to Recover

For many of us, the first landmark of financial recovery is anger. We are angry that we cannot spend freely. We are often angry at our significant others, as they may fight our newly found solvency with demands that we continue to spend as before. It takes courage to recover from codependent spending.

NOVEMBER 11

Masks

Money madness is a disease of masks. Our unmanageability frequently changes shape. We may first identify as a chronic spender, then realize we have issues with cash codependency. The mask slips again as we recognize our bouts as money misers, and yet again as big deal chasers or maintenance managers. Asking for spiritual help, we begin to address all of our toxic behaviors.

NOVEMBER 12

Solvency as Self-Respect

Often, we tell ourselves "If I had more money, I would have more respect." We set a magic number that we believe will earn us esteem. But the respect that truly matters is self-respect, and that comes to us through solvency.

NOVEMBER 13

Money as Love

Many of us grew up with the toxic belief that money equaled love. Spending became how we expressed our affection. We needed, always, to spend more, to buy our place in the hearts of others.

November 14

Work as Love

The workaholic buys the message "work is love." But hours spent on the job are often hours denied to loved ones. Solvency brings intimacy. The workaholic learns to express true love through time spent.

Compassion for Ourselves

One of the first fruits of solvency is compassion. The first place we must practice compassion is with ourselves. We must dismantle our perfectionism and learn to settle for progress, not perfection.

Money as Social Standing

Many of us have bought the toxic belief that money equals social standing. Believing that rich equals smart, we believe that if we could just have "more," we could buy people's respect.

A New Walk

As we source ourselves in Spirit and begin to work
with solvency tools, we experience the breaking up of
old and toxic habits. With Spirit as our source, we are
given the strength to walk a new walk.

NOVEMBER 18

Entitlement

For many of us, our chronic financial mismanagement begins with a feeling of entitlement. The world owes us a living, we feel. The world owes us more than what we have.

NOVEMBER 19

Financial Heroism

Many of us indulge in overspending as a form of financial heroism. Our grandiosity demands that we spend beyond our means. We often spend to rescue others, mistaking their gratitude for love.

November 20

Moral Compass

Money madness often robs us of our morals. With money as the be-all and end-all, it is often used as the sole variable in making complex decisions. We go where the money is, not where our moral compass may point us.

A Family Secret

Many of us grow up with money as a family secret. Discussion of money is taboo. We never really know how much we have, how much we need, how much we can rely on.

NOVEMBER 22

Bargains

Often we spend—and overspend—because an item is on sale and "a great buy." We may not need the item at all, but we cannot resist the siren song of a bargain.

Discomfort

Financial mismanagement causes stress, and stress causes financial mismanagement. We act out in toxic ways to alleviate our feelings of discomfort. As we do so, our discomfort increases.

The Big Deal

If our money mismanagement takes the form of big deal chasing, we seek a windfall that is sudden and huge. We have no patience for gradual improvement. We are addicted to the fantasy of the dramatic "win."

A Vicious Cycle

Many of us are addicted to anxiety. We lack the clarity that brings serenity. Our terminal vagueness regarding our finances creates stress. Stress is the invitation to act out. Acting out creates more anxiety. It is a vicious cycle.

November 26

The Drama of Debt

Financial mismanagement creates drama. Accustomed
to stress, we act out in ways that increase our anxiety.
Solvency, with its calm and serenity, seems very foreign to us. We often elect drama just because it is fa-
miliar. By its very nature, debt is dramatic.

Liar, Liar

Terminal vagueness tells us our finances are okay when they are not. Terminal vagueness tells us this time will be different when it won't. When we hit bottom, we realize that terminal vagueness is a liar. We experience the realization that we are truly powerless in financial matters. "Help me," we plead to Spirit. Our denial shatters. We become willing to take our first steps toward solvency.

November 28

The Cycle of Shame

Financial mismanagement breeds shame. Shame, in turn, breeds financial mismanagement. Turning to Spirit, we experience our first glimmering of self-worth. We learn compassion. As we act responsibly, self-worth replaces shame.

The American Dream

Money madness feeds on the American Dream. That dream is comprised half of money and half of fame. When we pursue either for itself alone, we fall prey to toxic behaviors.

November 30

Affirmative Prayer

Sourced in Spirit, we can practice affirmative prayer.
We do not petition Spirit for its help; we affirm that we
receive it.

December

DECEMBER 1

Financial Anorexia

Money madness takes many forms. Financial anorexia is one of them. We refuse to deal with money, so we underearn and underspend. We get "high" on our lack of money.

Workaholism

To recover from money madness, many of us need to recover from workaholism. We find we work unreasonable hours, often for unreasonable pay. In recovery, we value our time and energy. We work normal hours for normal pay.

Borrowing

Borrowing from our family, friends, and employers is a common form of debting. We confuse money with love, and when we borrow, we feel loved by the lender. Often we have no real plan for repayment. We feel entitled to the cash.

December 4

Acting Out

When we set a bottom line on our financial behaviors, we set a boundary. We will no longer indulge toxic behaviors in ourselves or others. We stop acting out.

December 5

Childhood Patterns

As money-mad adults, many of us find we are reenacting childhood patterns with money. We beg, borrow, and steal in order to feel loved. Our relationship to money is not rational.

DECEMBER 6

Pain

Very often, pain is what causes us to hit bottom on financial mismanagement. Our behaviors are toxic and cause us suffering. Our denial finally shatters, and we find ourselves begging for spiritual help. We have hit bottom.

DECEMBER 7

A New Perception

Sourced in Spirit, we experience a new perception of ourselves. Our worth is not synonymous with our net worth. We have value and dignity apart from our financial bottom line.

December 8

Change for the Better

Toxic stress is the prelude to acting out. In recovery, we experience a new, nontoxic stress: the stress of change. As we set a bottom line and stick to it, we experience change for the better.

DECEMBER 9

Character

Money mad, we pursue the dollar as social standing.
Solvent, we find our worth springs from our character,
not our bank account.

December 10

Goals and Dreams

When we are money mad, our goals are often pie-in-the-sky. In recovery, one doable step at a time, our goals are more realistic. Solvent, we are often able to achieve goals and dreams that have eluded us.

DECEMBER 11

Right-Sized

Sourced in Spirit, we eschew grandiosity and embrace humility. We become right-sized. We find ourselves more comfortable in our skin. No longer showing off, we embrace realistic goals, winning the respect of ourselves and others.

December 12

Money Is Neutral

Often, when we are money misers, we carry an unconscious belief that money is evil. Money is not evil, money is not good. Money is neutral.

Imagination as Ally

During money madness, many of us abused our imaginations, creating toxic, grandiose visions of the future. In establishing solvency, our imagination becomes an ally and an asset. We visualize the future grounded in dignity. We use our imagination to achieve our goals a step at a time.

DECEMBER 14

Money Mapping

Counting is a daily tool. Money mapping is a monthly
tool. The Prosperity Plan is built on a solid foundation
of both tools. Money mapping is where our money
does go. The Prosperity Plan is where our money could
go. As the two converge, we find ourselves experienc-
ing financial health.

DECEMBER 15

A Habit of Worry

In practicing money madness, many of us become habituated to adrenaline, habituated to a habit of worry.
Our finances are toxic and our terminal vagueness
keeps us off center. One of the first fruits of solvency
is clarity. We no longer worry needlessly. Counting,
we know how much money we have and where it
should go.

December 16

Credit Cards

For all of their convenience, credit cards are a threat to solvency. They should be used only if paid off immediately; otherwise, debt can occur. Credit card roulette is a common malady: loading up one card and then moving on to the next.

DECEMBER 17

Intimidation

When we are money mad, we are often bullied. Intimidation is a routine threat to our serenity. We fear
the phone; we fear mail. We feel guilty and ashamed.
Our self-worth is minimal. Solvent, we cease to be
intimidated. We face our debts and live within our
means.

DECEMBER 18

Money as God

Our dollar bill states "In God We Trust," but when we are money mad, we trust the dollar itself. We trust money as God, putting our faith in our bank balance rather than in Spirit. When we debt, we feel damned.

DECEMBER 19

Letting Go of Fear

Sourced in Spirit, committed to solvency, we find ourselves letting go of fear. Dread and apprehension no longer are our daily companions. Optimism and hope take their place.

The Spiral of Debt

Living beyond our means, many of us are caught up in the spiral of debt. We live in ways we cannot afford. We tell ourselves such living is "normal."

Destructive Spending

When we spend beyond our means, we are engaged in what might be called "destructive spending." It threatens our self-worth. We jeopardize our future.

December 22

An End to Clutter

Money mad, we procrastinate. We don't open the mail.
We don't return calls. Our homes become filled with
clutter. Amidst the debris, it is hard to think clearly.
Solvent, we begin to become current. We sort through
clutter until we find clarity. Once found, we keep our
affairs in order.

Our Earnest Efforts

Solvent, sourced in Spirit, we learn compassion. Rather than fall victim to perfectionism, we instead appreciate our earnest efforts.

Safeguarding Our Future

Calling our savings "freedom accounts," we learn to safeguard our future. We have cash on hand to meet emergencies. We have the freedom to not worry.

December 25

Baby Steps

When we stop debting and start solvency, we begin by small steps. Little changes make a big difference. Our Prosperity Plan is built on tiny changes.

December 26

Buying Love

Believing money equals love, lending money is a toxic pattern for many of us. We believe that a timely loan will buy us love. Conversely, we are often afraid to say "no" when asked for money.

Self-Forgiveness

One of the first fruits of solvency is self-forgiveness. As we take daily steps toward our financial health, we no longer indulge in self-loathing. We no longer beat ourselves up. We now have the capacity to make wise choices.

Order

Money mad, our lives are chaotic. Debris accumulates. Cleaning up our financial debris, we get current and stay current. Solvent, our lives become orderly.

A Reasonable Plan

Debt repayment is an important part of solvency. Abstinent, no longer debting, we need to make a reasonable plan to repay monies owed. It is important that we not promise more than we can spare. Creating a reasonable plan, we are able to fulfill our promise. Our self-worth builds.

DECEMBER 30

Safe in Emergencies

Ten percent of monies in must go to our freedom account. Although it seems small, it builds rapidly. Freedom accounts keep us safe in emergencies.

Abundance

When we believe in an abundant Universe, we are able to receive prosperity as a spiritual gift. Our abundance harms no one. Rather, it sets an example for others to follow.

If you enjoyed this book, visit

www.tarcherbooks.com

and sign up for Tarcher's e-newsletter to receive
special offers, giveaway promotions, and
information on hot upcoming releases.

TARCHER
PENGUIN

Great Lives Begin with Great Ideas

Connect with the Tarcher Community

• • •

Stay in touch with favorite authors!
Enter weekly contests!
Read exclusive excerpts!
Voice your opinions!

Follow us

 Tarcher Books

@TarcherBooks

If you would like to place a bulk order
of this book, call 1-800-847-5515.

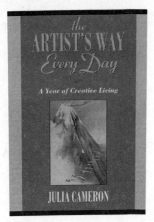

From the author of the international bestseller *The Artist's Way*, a daily guide to cultivating a deeper connection with your creative self

978-1-58542-747-5
$14.95

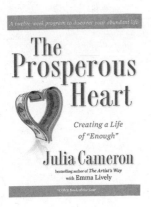

"Inspiring stories of how money affects people's lives accompany tools, exercises, and strategies for discovering the true meaning of prosperity and abundance in this uplifting and beneficial guide."

—*Publishers Weekly*

978-0-399-16198-8
$17.95